Puppets and Marionettes

Raymond Humbert

Translated by Juliet Peters

A Magnet Book

The antique puppets which feature in this book are exhibited
at the Musee Rural des Arts Populaires de Laduz (Yonne).
They are part of Raymond Humbert's personal collection.
The children's puppets which feature in this book were
made at the Ecole des Beaux Arts D'Auxerre, in the workshops
of Marie-Jose Drogou, Martine Gollot, and Jaqueline
and Jean-Christophe Humbert. Photographs by Marie-Jose Drogou.

First published in Great Britain in 1988
by Methuen Children's Books Ltd
Michelin House, 81 Fulham Road,
London SW3 6RB
Copyright © 1987 by Dessain et Tolra, Paris
English translation by Juliet Peters
Copyright © 1988 Methuen Children's Books

Printed in Italy
by Tipolitografia G. Canale & C. S.p.A. - Turin
ISBN 0 416 12922 6

Contents

1. The spirit of puppets   4

2. Puppets throughout the world   6

3. Puppets throughout history   8

4. Variety of puppets   19

5. Puppets for children   22
    Educational techniques   22
    Forming working groups   27
    Preparatory work   28
    Tools and materials   29
    Different approaches   30
    The Puppet Theatre and its Scenery   31
    The Text   35
    Development of techniques   37
    Finger puppets   37
    Hand puppets   43
    Rod puppets   45
    Jumping Jacks, flat moving puppets   54
    Chinese shadow puppets   59
    Glove puppets   65
    Rod and string puppets   68

6. Puppets for adults   70
    Motivation and field of action   70
    Diversity of techniques   75
    How to enjoy puppets   76
    Summing up the role of puppetry   77

1. *The spirit of puppets*

Puppetry is a medium. Through this medium it is possible to explore all the basic characteristics of human behaviour, while at the same time it gives us a chance to exagerate these characteristics and features so that we can take them forward into a world of fantasy. An example of this is the well known television programme 'Spitting Image', where the features and characters of well known personalities are exaggerated into a grotesque fantasy based on truth. This effect is reached by the rhythmic movements that the puppeteer uses to animate his puppets.

Unlike the actor who only plays one part, the puppeteer is responsible for far more. He must create the whole atmosphere for his puppets; the setting, the sound effects, the costumes, and all the background which enables the puppet to come alive. The puppet cannot exist without the appropriate setting, for example the booth or the screen for shadow puppets. The settings play an important part in creating the atmosphere of the show.

On the whole a puppet play is rather simple and direct. Like the pantomime, the simple plot gives a wide canvas for interpretation. The puppeteer has to set up a relationship with his audience, and it is this relationship which creates the atmosphere of the puppet play. The puppeteer is not only manipulating his puppets, he is at the same time manipulating his audience. He creates a mini world which communicates directly with them.

Adults have often found puppetry a problem. They find it hard to relate to the world of puppets which has a total disrespect for the conventions of real life, such as religion, respect for authority, and death. They tend to see puppets as props for children, rather like talking dolls, or cuddly mascots, and they think of puppet plays as being fairy tales, without realising the complexity and diversity of this art form.

Left
*The devil jumps from his box. The
element of surprise is important for
the dramatic effect it gives to the
story.*

Below
*Papier mâché clown. A simple toy
with separate hands cut out of
wood, and painted.*

Left, below
*A metal toy painted and animated
in the XIXth century. Note the expressive features of his face.*

2. Puppets throughout the world

These french wood and papier mâché puppets are reminiscent of the small statues of the virgin, and other minute religious figures found in the Middle Ages in France, or the mariolettes found in the XIXth century in Venice.

Puppets have always been found throughout the world, doubling as idols, masks and dolls. The Italians have many names for their puppets: pupi, pupazzi, fantocci, burattini, ancestors of the characters of the Commedia dell'Arte. Each country has its own puppets created from popular mythology. Don Christoval saves the day in Spain, Jean Saucisse heavy and loud in Germany, Casperle and Jean Klaassen in Holland, Mr Punch in England, the hideous Karageuz in Turkey. Japan and India also had their own puppets. Java and South America created their own characters, not forgetting China where the first puppets appeared a thousand years before Christ.

Although puppetry is international, the methods of making and using them are very different from one country to another. Some puppets have a sacred character and others are totally profane. Some puppet shows were designed for the popular masses, others for the courts or the drawing rooms. Their objectives were often totally opposed. Puppetry occupies a privileged place between the live theatre and the fairground.

Scraps of material are the starting point for marionettes. If one is patient and clever one can create some beautiful clothes. To paint the head, the eyes and the mouth, the paint must not be too diluted, otherwise it may fade.

Rich fabrics give these simple puppets a rich decorative effect. It is a good idea to match the fabric with the paint used. If the nose or the head are prominent, a little bit of material or tissue paper stuck on will give it that added volume.

Actual Spanish Puppets. The simple materials used to make the base work very well. If you are making this type of puppet it is better to make a paper model first.

3. Puppets throughout history

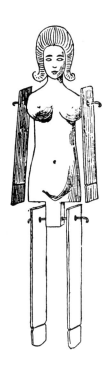

Many famous personalities from the past have used puppets to illustrate their work. Plato, Aristotle, Shakespeare, Voltaire, Byron and Goethe. Many famous celebrities have made and played with puppets such as George Sand, and the artists Bonnard, Vuillard and Paul Klee. Many others have been close to them; Fernand Leger, Miro, Calder and Picasso made carved dolls for their children.

Puppets have formed their culture from many aspects of life such as science, art, poetry, religion and politics. They have acquired their form from sculpture, their colour from art, their movement from engineering, their words from poetry and prose, while song and dance have brought them to life. Finally, improvisation, the most precious gift of all, has given them the liberty of free speech.

In the XVIth century mathematicians were fascinated by their movement, as were musicians like Hayden. The puppets at that time were made of wood, bone, ivory, clay, cardboard, or simply of cloth representing real and fictional characters, and animated by strings, springs or metal wires, all operated by the invisible hand.

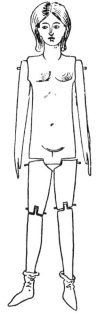

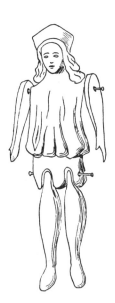

Illustrations showing moving dolls prominent in Greek sculpture. These statues are an early example of moving characters, possibly props of the Greek theatre.

Right
The line between sculpture and puppetry is very finely drawn. Here is a virgin and child made of chromium plated wood made in the XVIIIth century. They were dressed in clothes which were changed with the liturgical calendar.

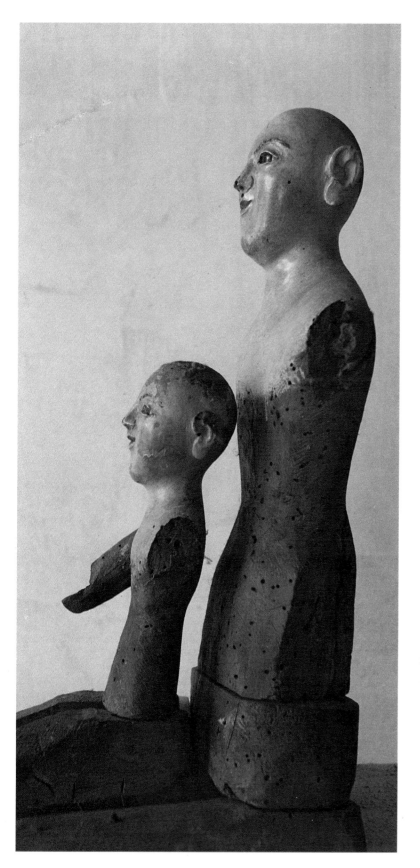

Puppets are contemporary with the first little girl inventing the doll, a miniature example of herself. An object of love and caring, the doll also gives the child a chance to play the role of her mother giving the orders and expecting obedience. The doll enlivens the spirit. The rattle which diverts the child's attention away from her anger or tears, thus becomes an influence and acquires the role of a puppet.

The puppet was also born from a tiny piece of clay or wood being formed into an idol. This idol would then be painted, dressed, covered in flowers, shells or jewels, and brought gifts in the hope that wishes would be granted. After having given them the appearance of life, they were carved to seem as if they had power and movement, thus giving them the semblance of responding. The lines between men and gods was therefore very finely drawn. From this last stage moving sculpture was born, completing the illusion of life. These illusions were achieved in two ways, one was achieved with springs hidden inside the statue and animated when necessary, the other with wires or strings attached to the limbs and manipulated. Before becoming the priority of children in the town squares and market places, puppets had their place in the temples and holy places. Christian art followed down the same route as paganism.

A wood engraving from the Middle Ages depicting the making of toys and puppets.

In ancient Egyptian literature, particularly the book of Herod written for the celebration of the birthday of Osiris, there is mention of moving statues. Then from the ancient Greeks we learn that the gold statue of Apollo moved itself using springs. At Preneste, the famous statue of Juno and Jupiter as children sitting on the knee of Fortune, their nurse, was said to have moved. Early Greek meals were often enlivened with a puppet show, and spring statues were much prized. It was the same in early Roman times. The actors of Sophocles and Eurypedes were themselves partly made of wood, walking on a type of stilt and with the forearms and hands enlarged by a false piece. Most puppets that we have seen from the past are very similar to modern puppets.

Puppets are, by the very way they are made, a parody of human life. It also is this parody which has probably fed and added to the variety of the repertoire in all countries. No doubt the actors in Athens enriched their repertoire at the expense of the politicians, philosophers and writers, much to the delight of their audience.

Reproduction of a work from the Middle Ages. Young children playing soldiers, using puppets.

Reproduction of a movable Punch
from the Directoire period.

One of the favourite themes from the beginning of theatre scripts has been the exposure of all that is ridiculous and unfair in society. Puppets follow this form of theatre with its world of fantasy, caricature and masks. In times gone by the antics of these artificial actors seemed minor compared to the cruel reality presented in the arenas and the live theatre.

Subsequently Christian art continued to develop the moving statue following exactly the same route as pagan art. If the first Christians expressed their beliefs in symbolic form, Christianity emerged from the catacombs to develop its religious rites. Saint

Gregory and Saint Thomas declared that it was praiseworthy to use intelligence and art to elevate the spirit, by substituting images for realism. The madonnas that have been restored have stomachs that open to reveal the baby Jesus. They dressed them and covered them with jewels, then moved them with wires and springs, thus creating a new type of idol. Even today the little angels round the manger bow their heads when money is inserted. These mechanical sculptures were often thought to be magic.

One finds in puppets the characters from everyday life, either fantasy or real. Pierrot meets Mother Michel and the "Pioupiou", a soldier, around 1900.

Characters on parade waiting for action. Their heads are made of papier mâché, their clothes are made of special cloth. They were sold in different sized boxes. They had painted hands, and different expressions painted on their faces.

Opposite page
If Guignol had known how to defend himself he would have confronted the judge, the policeman, the devil, or any combination of foes. His red face and clothes evoke the flames of hellfire.

Processions were an excuse for using large puppets, partly religious, partly popular. Mysticism and carnival were often mixed together. The mythical characters of each city or region, such as the dragon of Paris slewn by Saint Michael, were paraded through the streets spreading feelings of awe and terror. The terrified, excited people would throw money, sweets, cakes and flowers in the path of these giant puppets. It was not only dragons and monsters represented in these parades, but also giants such as Goliath and St Christopher. Puppets were a part of the mystery plays which took place in the cathedral squares. The prestige of moving sculpture designed to stir the hearts of the faithful, was an important part of the culture found in France, Italy, and Spain, where religious plays were presented at fairs.

Right
Guignol, between the judge and the policeman from the Lyon puppet theatre, at the end of the XIXth century. You can see here the skill with which they were painted. The expressions on their faces, and the characteristics of their heads are cleverly executed.

The policeman, the judge, the cat and Pierrot, are gathered together here. They only await a child to come alive. Dating about 1900, they are simple but effective, and could still hold their own today.

Opposite
Colour is most important in puppetry. The colour is tied up with the celebration, The emphasis is given by the directness of style.

Below
Papier Mâché has given birth to many puppet heads. Drying slowly it can easily be modelled into shape. Paint emphasises the features. A coat of varnish gives it the strength and endurance to withstand the rigours of the action.

It is difficult to say at what stage the word 'Marionette' began to refer to something other than a doll. It seems to have been around the period of 1584. There seem to have been puppet theatres around at that period. The puppets of the XVth and XVIth centuries, following their traditional role, seem to have been based on the comic or grotesque characters of the time. Eventually, under Henry IV, they adopted the names of Harlequin, Pantalon, Punchinelle and Pierrot.

14

Cardboard puppets 1890-1900. The features were made to resemble well known personalities.

Wooden headed puppets from the theatre Lyonnaise. Guignol and the policemen are in continual conflict.

From 1649 to 1697 the popular puppets of the Pont Neuf in Paris were famous thanks to the Brioché family who combined dentistry with puppeteering. They presented the Combat de Cyrano de Bergerac. In 1669 at the birth of Tartuffe, Brioché was invited to play for the Dauphin at the court of St Germain en Laye. After puppetry entered court it became a popular entertainment in the drawing rooms. They also appeared at the opera and the Comédie Française. Puppets appeared at all the fairs, and the loves of Policinelle were among the biggest crowd gatherers. In 1784 a new pleasure centre was built for the people of Paris. A permanent Fair was built at the Palais Royal. Brioché and his Théâtre des Pygmées was a permanent attraction. They later moved to the boulevards, the squares and public gardens.

The beginning of the XIXth century heralded a renaissance for puppetry. For centuries, there had been troups of puppets travelling in their own regions, with their own traditions and methods. This was so in Lyon, where a poverty stricken artist who had been a dentist, Laurent Mourguet, invented Guignol in 1795. Guignol with his good sense, his feeling of equality, his fight against the privileged classes, he symbolised the struggle of the working man against blind power. His wife Madelon, his boss Battandier, the wicked Canezou, and Gnafron, all take part in the life of Guignol.

4. Variety of puppets

The purpose of puppets is the life that one can give them. To achieve this there are two main forms of manipulation. Puppets moved from above, and those moved from beneath. The oldest form were the rod puppets. They probably originate from the bells they used to dangle in front of babies, which later became dangling dolls. They probably also derive from the bells carried by the king's fools. The simplest form of rod puppet is a simple rod which is attached to the body. The more complicated examples had rods attached to all their limbs. The puppets thus floated in space.

This form of animation spread during the XIIIth century from Java. It was called *Wayang Golek* and *Wayang Keroutyll*, and later was found in Siam and Bali. Some puppets were fixed to a base and only the arms moved. Rod puppets were also popular in Belgium and Sicily.

Rod puppets were succeeded by string puppets. They were moved in a similar fashion depending on the number of strings. They had the advantage of making the movements more realistic. All these were made from a body of wood shaped like a cross. The Salzburgh puppets are a good example of this method. In America humans play the part of the puppet, as can be seen in the large fairs such as Disneyland, where the enormous heads and hands are made of cardboard or papier mâché.

Glove puppets are manipulated from below, the puppeter working beneath the puppet. The heads of glove puppets are made of wood, paper or card, and the bodies are made of cloth. The puppets are activated by the hand with fingers taking the place of the puppet's hands. These puppets are presented in a booth with scenery and lighting which changes with the story being told.

Shadow theatre is one of the most ancient forms of puppetry. It comes from the Orient and has achieved great popularity in Europe. Behind a thin screen hung from a brightly lit frame, one can make these puppets move in many ways. The shadow puppets can be made of papier mâché, wood or laminated metal, they are attached to boards and animated with the use of sticks or metal rods.

Above
Knitted puppets, carefully knitted in a pull-over pattern to give a sense of life.

Left
Moving toys have always existed. By 1900 they had reached the height of their popularity and were extremely cleverly made as you can see from the examples on this page.

A very simple form of this was found in the shooting galleries at the fairgrounds in the XIXth century. By an ingenious system of pulleys and cables, the head was shot off the victim! They saw at these fairgrounds, the avenging newly weds, the return of the soldier, the brave fireman and, of course, Pierrot and Columbine. The public demand for emotional stimulation was gratified, and public opinion could often be influenced by the stories they watched.

Pierrot and Columbine are the most popular of puppet characters. They are also famous in songs and poetry where they have a gentle poetic image.

In France during the XIXth century the majority of marionette theatres were in Paris, but there were at least thirty troups of puppeteers travelling throughout the country. The booths were often about 25 metres long, and the front was very brightly painted. The plays were mostly of Mr Punch and his misdemeanours, and the charge for entry varied from about two sous to one franc. When the troup arrived in a new town they would rush round hanging posters, and then parade through the town carrying puppets and banging drums and tambourines to publicise themselves. There would be at least one performance a day, and sometimes on Sunday there would be three or four. Each group would consist of at least ten people, six puppeteers, two scenic artists, a carpenter and of course a musician.

The stories presented during the XIXth century were all based on the same ideas, with slight variations according to regional changes. The stories catered for all emotional tastes and the puppet theatre was an extremely popular form of entertainment.

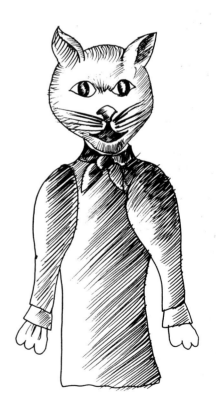

5. *Puppets for children*

Reproduction of a Guignol theatre in 1900. The Devil and Punch fight it out as the orchestra plays beneath them.

Educational techniques

Before we start it is important to understand the role of puppets.

If puppets were invented by adults, they were soon taken over by children because of their similarity to dolls. Most children, and even some adults, play at puppets without realising they are doing so. How many of us have created a character out of an object, such as a twig, an old sock or even a piece of food? Children often act out their fantasies using their hands as characters, and they can often solve their innermost problems by using their hands and fingers to play the part of their adversary.

The creation of a puppet, therefore, is not only the creation of an object but also a personality. You can endow your puppet with any emotion or sentiment you wish. Puppetry, if you think about it carefully, has an unique place as an art form. It combines art, sculpture, writing, speech and music into a total theatrical experience, which is both educational and entertaining.

Puppetry can be the way for a child to begin to understand how people feel. It also gives him the chance to create and direct something for himself, and also to work as part of a team.

The group will need to discuss their story and characters, and this can be an important lesson in listening to one another. They also have to learn to communicate with their audience. They can explore real life situations through their stories, and can dip back into the past, or project themselves into the future. There are therefore two roles for puppetry to play in the cultural development of a child.

The first is the making of the puppet, the second is to bring it alive and make it communicate with an audience. The most important rule for artistic expression is to allow each child to experiment, expand and discover for himself. It is important to encourage them to observe and to use their imaginations. It is important also to look at other people's work and to learn how certain effects have been created.

The child's imagination knows no boundaries, and carries on far beyond the standard choices of colour and materials and technique usually offered. Fine art is created to last for generations to come, and therefore the materials used are chosen accordingly. The sculptor will tend to use durable materials such as stone, bronze, gold or silver. Popular art on the other hand, tends to use materials that are a part of life, such as wood, string or cloth. If fine art is created to be looked at, such as the painting, or the statue in the square, popular art is made for people to use. The statue in the square has descended from his pedestal and become the dancing marionette. Marionettes are a supreme example of popular art. They rely on materials which are readily available in everyday life, and are often free or extremely cheap to acquire. Made from wood or papier mâché they are dressed using scraps of material or old clothes, and decorated with string, straw, feathers, old bits of fur, or any scraps that might be suitable to create an effect. Old buttons can be used for eyes, or even as medals for a brave soldier.

The story of Little Red Riding Hood and the big bad wolf has gripped many generations of children. Fairy tales do not only exist in books, but have been the inspiration of many puppet plays.

In our modern consumer age, we can find much more material to use than at the beginning of the century. One just needs to keep all the packaging that would normally be thrown away. What a feast of materials we now have at our disposal. The range is unending, cotton reels, corrugated cardboard, shoe and matchboxes, but particularly the plastic matter; yoghourt cartons, bottle tops, polystyrene, and polyester which one can find in leaves, cubes or moulded pieces.

In addition to the range of materials now offered to us, there are the traditional materials that have been used in the past, and can be found throughout the world. Bird feathers, or even painted feathers, twigs, branches, seeds, and vegetables such as the carrot or the pumpkin. String or cotton allow us to tie on costumes or props, while the slipper, the glove and the sock are indispensible. The modern puppeteer therefore has a continuous source of materials at his disposal.

Paper plates, egg boxes, and plastic bottles have their own particular designs which can suggest all sorts of creative ideas. The work of art can therefore be shaped by the diversity of materials available.

Left
Clowns have fascinated children through the ages. Puppet shows in fairgrounds were often based on the circus.
A romantic lithograph showing children playing with a jumping jack.

Above
Chromolithograph of the XIXth century. To understand the evolution of puppet making it is important to study the design, method, and animation used throughout the centuries.

*Engraving from a catalogue
dating from 1900.*

The puppet has its place somewhere between the Christian or pagan statue, the straight theatre, and the fairground. The art of puppetry grew during the heyday of the carnival, dying off for a time with it's demise. The way a puppet is moved can convey an emotion or a human attribute which will communicate itself to the audience. This ability is based not only on imaginative skill, but also on a technique which has been carefully learned. Once the skill has been learned, it can be applied and adapted to be used within the artistic interpretation. There are several different techniques which can be applied depending on the materials that have been used.

A puppet can be a representation of a true character, a fictional character or even of an idea or an emotion such as anger, pride or fear. The character of the puppet can be embellished not only by the conception of it's character, but also by the methods and use of material when it is created. String used as hair can define a character purely by the amount that is used. A potato cut into the right shape, painted with a metal paint, and decorated with pins and bottle tops, becomes a robot.

The choice of materials for the costume is also important in determining the character. Finally the movements used; gentle and smooth for the goody, harsh and jerky for the baddie.

The text can be seen as an accompaniment to the story. It provides the familiar repetition of words and the sound effects. The life of the marionette can be different. Some only exist for the moment, such as finger or hand puppets, or indeed those we create out of a fork, a twig or an article of clothing. Others have been fashioned out of materials which are guaranteed to withstand the rigours of professional life. The plays are repeated time after time, sometimes several times a day and although the odd scene may be changed a little here and there, the basic stories have existed and delighted audiences throughout the generations. It is their very repetitiveness which holds the secret of their appeal.

Forming working groups

Before setting up a working group it is important to take several things into consideration. The age and abilities of the children being the first consideration. Some may be artistic and will enjoy designing the puppets and scenery. The more practical ones will enjoy implementing the designs and deciding which are the best materials to use. Imaginative children will enjoy discussing the story and writing the text. A group of about ten children with a good balance of interests and abilities is ideal to start a successful working team.

A good space is essential to work in. It is fun to have several puppets on the go at once so that the children can begin to get to know their characters.

Preparatory work

Before embarking on the making of puppets it is important to plan your working space. As well as the working area you will need storage space for materials and tools as well as somewhere to keep the puppets and the puppet theatre.

You will need large tables, the best are collapsable trestles, as they are ideal for storage, so that there is plenty of room for each child to work. These can be covered in thick card to prevent any damage when cutting out the puppets. Plastic cloths should also be available for use during painting. The tables should be placed in a good light so that the children are not bothered by shadows when working. The children should be asked to wear overalls or old clothes that can be soiled. There should be a source of water nearby, and sufficient pots for everyone. Yoghourt pots and the bottom halves of plastic bottles are ideal for this. The materials neccesary for making the puppets can be accumulated gradually with the help of the children.

Before the children start making the puppets it is important that they are given the practical details they need to know. The materials they can use, how to use them best, the tools and methods of using them, the method and length of the drying process, and the best means of decoration, must be known to them before they can let their imaginations take over.

On this workbench, heads made of modelling clay have had paper glued on, and then painted.

Tools and materials

The tools you are going to use must be gathered together, taking care to omit anything that is too dangerous or toxic. For the sake of economy glue and paint should be bought carefully. Large tubes of both are ideal. You will need lots of different sized brushes, wide paint brushes for large surfaces down to fine brushes for painting in features. You will need several different types of glue, suitable for the materials you are using. A cutter is essential but should only be used under supervision.

It is extremely important to establish an order of work so that children can explore one possibility thoroughly before moving on to the next. That way they do not become confused and are motivated to move on to the next stage having thoroughly appreciated the previous one. The course should not always be rigid, allowing the children to explore and expand the knowledge they are gaining. It is an advantage to have a radiator or heater of some sort to hasten the drying process. This way the children will not get too bored and lose their motivation.

Here are some materials ready for use. Modelling clay which can be bought in several colours, modelling tools in wood or plastic, then finally the paper, cardboard and glue to fix the face on to paste or clay.

A simple cone becomes Father Christmas with just a dash of paint and some cotton wool.

Different approaches

Having taken account of the different ages, levels and abilities, it is important to decide what technique you are going to teach. It is best to start with a simple method that they can easily implement and quickly achieve a result. They will then gain the confidence to move on to a more difficult technique. The finger puppet can lead on to the hand puppet and then on to the more complicated forms. At each stage however, it is important that the children realise why they have created the puppet. It must, even in the early stages, be apparent to them that they are creating a theatrical experience of their own. At each stage therefore the experience must lead from the design and making of the puppets through to the final performance in an appropriate setting.

The action of life, represented by silhouettes moved by the children themselves. The spectators are masks made of polystyrene like the players.

The use of space is an important function of the puppet. In this picture you can see the small polystyrene faces (which hang as leaves from trees) which emphasise the height of the other characters. There is hardly any need for a story in this picture!

The Puppet Theatre and its scenery

Characters and decor are intimately linked during a performance, and it is important that they do not overule each other.

The puppet theatre is where the characters will come alive. It is neccesary to take into consideration the size of the puppets, and also the size of the spectators. The spectator must be able to concentrate without being distracted by the environment. The scene must be the centre of attention. The opening where the puppets are operated must be masked from the audience so that the operators' hands are not a distraction.

The theatre can be improvised. For example, two chairs placed about a metre apart, balanced on some books to give added height, and draped with a curtain, can give a good enough venue for a puppet play. The puppeteer has to kneel in order not to be seen. A door frame with the lower part covered can also work quite well. If you are working outdoors, a piece of material draped between two trees can work extremely well. The puppeteer must have his puppets in the right order so that he can pick them up as and when they are needed.

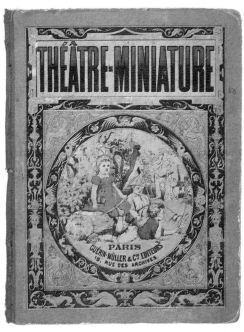

Left
The cover of a book on the history of Punch in the Champs-Elysées in 1900. Puppetry was very popular at this time and could be seen in the streets and the fairgrounds, as well as the more fashionable environments.

Opposite
Puppet theatres were also important and could be found advertised in the catalogues of fashionable shops. They were works of art in themselves as can be seen in this picture.

Childrens' books were beautiful during this period. In this example the scenes and the characters could be moved and changed to provide different stories.

In the case of rod puppets handled from below, it is a good idea to store them in a bottle perhaps partly filled with sand so that they can be firmly fixed. For very small puppets moved by fingers a shoe box makes an ideal puppet theatre. The puppeteer's hand is hidden and the audience can only see the fingers.

The more complex theatres are made from three hinged screens. The centre screen is wider than the two side screens. They are usually made of plywood and ideally can be folded away when not in use.

The scenery forms an integral part of the puppet theatre. It will differ from play to play, and even from scene to scene. First it is neccessary to create a screen at the front of the theatre which will hide the entrances and the exits of the puppets. They must be made of strong material, paper stuck on material, painted oilskin, thick cardboard, or even plywood. Once you have created the impression of depth, you can allow the decor to express the feeling and character of the play. If the puppets and the decor retain the same style it makes the play far more effective.

To make the play more interesting it is nice to have new scenery for each scene. You need to take account of the space required by the characters, the decor must not mask the action. In order that the interest of the audience is not lost during the scene changes they must be extremely quick. Rods fixed to the top of the screen which fit in to notches set at the sides of the theatre are ideal, as these can be slotted in quickly. If the scenery is not hand painted it can be made from a collage of photographs and materials stuck on to the screen to create an atmosphere. Do not use figures as part of a background as their immobility is distracting.

The text

The creation of puppets uses a selection of skills and artistic techniques which ends with the creation of a character or group of characters. Having given them a physical being they now need to be given words and action.

As the children are making the puppets they will begin to relate to them. They will have conversations with them and begin to give them an identity. Some children will be more imaginative than others and will already be imagining their puppets in various different situations. It is the function of the teacher at this point to listen carefully to the ideas, discuss them with the children and to sort them into an order from which they can begin to make their own play using the characters they have created for themselves.

Opposite page
Round about 1900 Japanese and Chinese art was discovered. Their brilliant use of light and shadow brought a new dimension to the Puppet Theatre.

Above
An example of Chinese shadow puppetry showing the World Exhibition in Paris in 1900. These toys were sold in the catalogues of the fashionable stores around 1900.

A cork, attached to a paper cone, is first painted white to make the puppet uniform. A few brush strokes, some pieces of string stuck on for whiskers and ears and you have a very realistic cat.

It is a good idea at this stage to try out lots of different ideas in order to see which the children like best.

While they are trying out their ideas the teacher can be taking notes. The ideas need to be written out so that the play has a good beginning, an orderly plot and a clear ending. It is preferable if as many ideas as possible can be incorporated into the plot, so that they all feel they have contributed something, however small.

When the plot has been decided it must be finalised so that each child knows the story thoroughly. Do not write a script giving each child specific lines, as this will take away the spontanaity of their words. It is important that the children communicate with the audience, and if they can use their own words without trying to remember lines, the charm of their own ideas will emerge.

Another way of working out a play is through the characters. Each child is responsible for his own character, and the relation the character would have to the story. The story can change according to the different reactions of the characters, which will then be discussed by the class until a final scenario is attained.

The play can be based on a story from a book, a poem, a work of art or entirely from the ideas of the children. Once the story has been devised it has to be formed into a play. The scenes need to be worked out taking into account the characters and their entrances and exits. This needs to be done carefully so that each scene is meaningful, and each character has a chance to communicate with the audience. The text, therefore, should be short, sharp, and to the point.

A scene should not last more than five minutes, and the whole play not longer than half an hour. A great deal is demanded of a group of children to create the puppets and their theatre, and then to devise the vehicle for their expression. They will, however, be more than amply rewarded by the tremendous sense of achievement that they will undoubtedly feel.

Development of techniques

Having discussed the history of puppets, the reasoning behind them, and the art as a whole, it is now time to study the different techniques of puppet making. As with all arts it is better to start with the simplest form. Once you have understood the logic behind the simpler forms, you are ready to graduate towards the more complex techniques. So we will start with the simple finger puppets, moving on to the hand puppets, the flat silhouettes, the moving silhouettes, the chinese shadows, glove and rod puppets moved from above and below, and string puppets. Each style is described in detail, from the techniques used, to the time and effort needed to make them. You need to decide if your play will work better with all the puppets being the same type, or whether different types of puppets would be more suitable for different characters. It is possible to have two versions of the same puppet so that it will seem to grow as the text demands.

Finger puppets

The finger has always been a method of communication between people. The mother waves her fingers at the baby as she sings him a cradle song, and disapproval is shown by the waving of one finger. These gestures with the fingers form the origin of using the fingers as puppets. These supple and flexible parts of the body are just waiting to be painted and dressed to become a character for themselves.

Cardboard box with two strips cut out to move the puppets.

Cardboard box with a back to paint and a front to hide the hands.

The painted finger

The advantage of this method is that you have almost instant results, and the children are immediately able to make their play and communicate with each other. A different character can be painted on each finger. The hand can disappear behind a table, a box or a bag. To make it look more exciting the fingers can be either the same colour, or a different colour for each one, and then the features and the clothes can be painted on top. A plastic bottle top or a feather can be used as a hat.

The theatre can be made from a cardboard box cut down to a size where the hand cannot be seen. Paint the box and put it on a table with a cloth over so that the puppeteer cannot be seen by his audience. You could even make a proper puppet theatre by folding or curving a piece of cardboard.

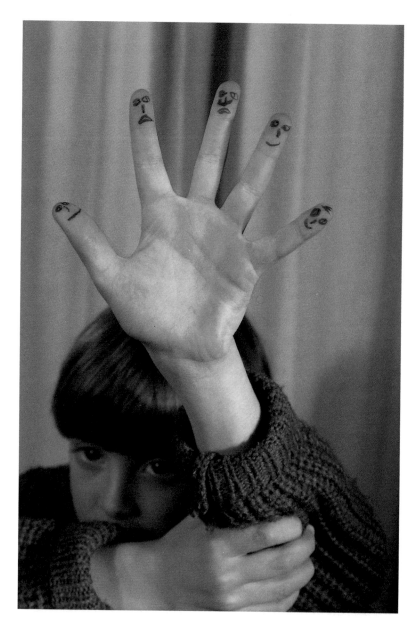

Useful materials

A cork is often a good starting point for a puppet. Take some thin card cut out a piece 4cm long and stick it round the cork for about half a centimetre, making a hollow cylinder that your finger can get inside. The head can be made from a champagne cork with a hat made from a piece of cork or a cone of paper.

Plastic gloves provide another source of puppet making. You can paint them, and unlike painting the fingers you do not have to wash the paint off so the puppets will last longer. You can stick any extras on with plastic glue.

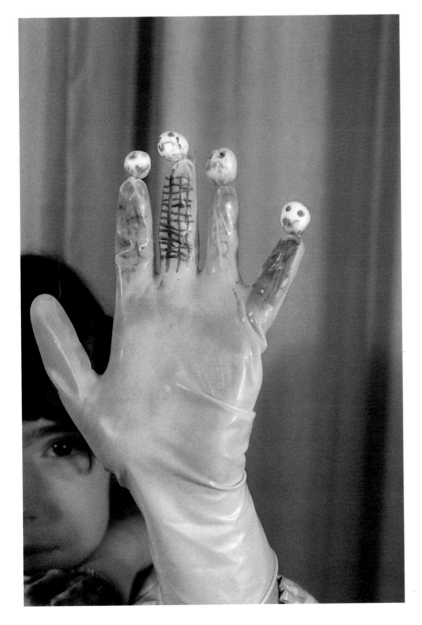

The ordinary cork creates a different shape from the Champagne cork. The extra bits stuck on emphasise their character.

A simple game is to create a character by painting the tip of your finger. It is possible in this simple way to communicate.

Here the fingers of a plastic glove become puppets. Bend your fingers and off you go. The heads could even be embroidered, and the costumes made from pieces of material.

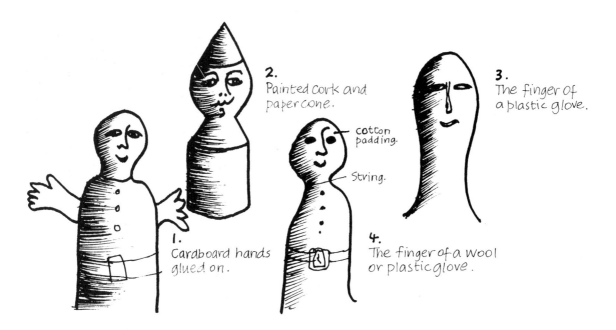

2.
Painted cork and paper cone.

cotton padding.

String.

3.
The finger of a plastic glove.

1.
Cardboard hands glued on.

4.
The finger of a wool or plastic glove.

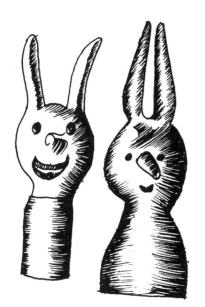

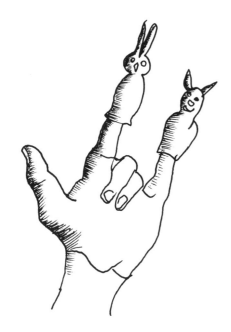

This type of puppet is perfect. The top can be separated from the rest with a piece of string, and the arms can be stuck on made from plastic or cardboard.

A slightly more complicated method is to make finger sized characters out of papier mâché. Cut up paper into narrow strips, any fine paper can be used such as newspaper, and soak it in water for several hours. If you are in a hurry soak it in hot water. While it is soaking make a small figure out of modelling clay the size of the finger. Equally you could make it out of a cylinder of card glued or pinned, or even sculptured out of a carrot or a potato. Having made your sculpture make the head, neck and arms by sticking on pieces of paper that have been coated in glue. Paper, wood or plastic glue can be used for this purpose. Take care that each piece overlaps the last following the shape of the sculpture. Brush each piece of paper with a glue brush after you have carefully put it in place. You will need three or four layers of paper to achieve the correct consistency. These puppets will need to be left to dry for several days. The process can be speeded up with the use of a hair dryer, a fan heater or a gas fire on low heat. Once dry you can add on the features with clay or modelling paste.

Finally comes the painting. Paint the whole puppet with a thick-base. When it has dried you can use the colours to paint in the relevant characteristics of your puppet, using the colour to highlight the features.

Another simple form of animation is to make a face out of a piece of card about 8-12 cms in diameter. Cut a hole where the nose should be, and use the finger to replace the nose and bring the puppet alive. The other features can be either painted or stuck on to give it depth.

A whole puppet can be made in a similar way. Cut the whole body out of cardboard and paint in the features. Where the legs should be, cut out two holes of about 0.5cms. The two fingers can be stuck through the holes to make legs. To make it even more realistic you can paint the legs. These puppets have the advantage of being almost instant. Puppets are relatively easily made this way and the children can have a great deal of fun working them.

The tongue passing through the mouth gives this puppet great personality. Two other fingers could be used to make the eyes and give an added effect.

The little half bodied puppets should be made in proportion to the fingers which will make the legs.

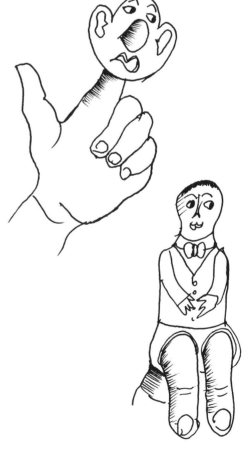

The painted hand. You can change the expressions on the face by moving the hands.

What fun to paint a person on your hand. You can make it look any way you like by just moving the palm. The fingers become hair, hat etc.

Hand puppets

Hands are an important and expressive part of the body. Physically they work for us and act as a form of communication with other people. There are several well known expressions about the hands. You give your hand in marriage, put your hands to work, and shake hands to make up a quarrel. As well as being useful and versatile physically therefore, the hand is very much considered to be part of our emotional life.

The hand is an incredible tool. One of the main features which make man superior to beast. Play with the painted hand! The puppet's face can be painted in the hollow of the hand or on the palm. If you paint a base on first it will accentuate the features, by slowly creasing the hand one can change the personality of the character. The fingers can be painted to represent the hair. If you wish it is possible to add accessories such as silver paper, or feathers.

Another form of puppet is the hand with fingers dressed up, or the fist covered in a mask of cardboard. Take care to measure the cardboard carefully before you cut it out. The features can be made out of paper or papier mâché and glued on. The thin cardboard of the face can be reinforced by a piece of firmer card, and it can be attached to the hand by a piece of elastic. The wrist becomes the neck of the puppet.

Simple heads for outdoor scenes.

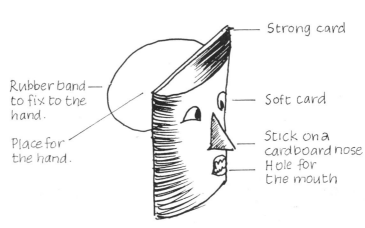

Rubber band to fix to the hand.

Place for the hand.

Strong card

Soft card

Stick on a cardboard nose
Hole for the mouth

The front of a wool or plastic glove makes an excellent puppet. On the woollen glove two buttons can be sewn on for eyes, and the mouth and nose can be sewn on in a contrasting colour. Plastic gloves are ideal as a base for puppets. Coloured felt is a brilliant way to bring them to life, along with other bits and pieces that can be glued on. From the glove you can move on to the old sock, and the old stocking. It is always wise to take the features of the basic material into consideration before planning the character that you are going to create.

The art of puppetry in the open air is based on simplicity. Here the simple cardboard head is attached to the sleeve of the puppeteer to make a simple but effective puppet.

Rod puppets

Which of us has not drawn a figure from our imagination on paper or in the sand, or indeed seen the shape of a character in the form of a cloud. This habit of drawing each other has dated from the earliest civilizations. The simplest forms are often the most evocative. The image sometimes preceeds a story, it fixes it in the memory, and in the world of puppets it is the starting point from which all the action springs. From the simple drawings emerge the living puppets.

Linear puppets

So many amazing things have been done in the past just by using a piece of wire. Famous sculptures made with just a profile, but giving the illusion of depth, are well known, and this method can also be effective in creating puppets.

It is fun to make linear puppets out of fine cardboard. Cut it into thin bands about 0.5cm, fold, bend and twist them into shape, and paint with thick glue to give them a figurative appearance. The characters can be of any size starting from about 5cms. They can be small enough to act in a theatre made of a shoe box, or can be as large as 50cms. Here the size of the expected audience can dictate the size of the puppets. The audience must be able to see the play. This method was used extensively in the XVIIth century when objects were made of rolled gold paper.

Graphic design is an ideal starting point for puppets made of wire or bands of paper, the features can be stuck on out of suitable bits of material.

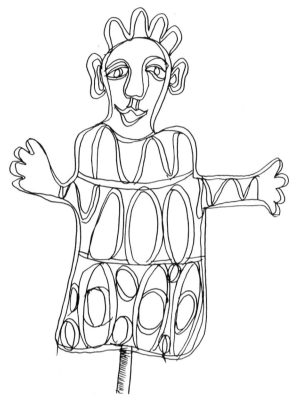

It is important to think carefully about the colour of the puppets. If they are just being used in space you can use almost any colour you like as long as it can be seen. If they are going to appear in a puppet theatre it is important they fit in with the decor, at the same time ensuring that they can be seen clearly. It is best to use contrasting colours, light colours on a dark background, and dark colours for a light background.

To make a simple but satisfactory cut-out silhouette puppet, paint a light colour on a dark base.

Flat puppets

Draw, colour or paint the character onto strong card before you cut it out. Make sure the silhouette is sharp. They are rather like weather vanes put on the roof of houses to tell the wind direction, but often giving a clue to the interest of the owner, for example, fishing or shooting. They can be given more relief by sticking on features such as an open mouth, or buttons, and can be livened up with props.

It is a good idea to study all the characters together. The colours and the style should be considered as a whole. The decor should also be considered and designed to blend with the style and colour of the puppets. The extra characters can sometimes be designed on one piece of card. A crowd scene for example can then be manned by one puppeteer, and a change of emotion by the crowd can be depicted on the other side of the card. They are all mounted on thin wooden rods about 40 to 50cms long.

The order in which the puppets are made must be strictly observed. They must be designed and then cut out. Don't fall into the trap of trying to make anything too large or too complicated.

The first stage is a rapid design which should be carefully coloured or painted, bearing in mind that you have to cut it out.

Right
These simple marionettes designed by children show all the imagination of the child with the delight they find in experimenting with colour.

The character of the puppet should start from the head. Here a painted cheese box is given hair made with curled paper. Next you make the neck followed by the rest of the body. The colours used give life to the marionette.

Solid puppets

These puppets have the advantage of looking more lifelike by the way they are made. We shall begin with the simplest forms, those made of paper or thin cardboard. Cones and cylinders are the geometric shapes most easy to make. They can be stuck together with glue, and mounted on a rod which serves both as a back, and a means of moving the puppet.

It will depend on the age of the children and the time available, whether you make very simple puppets or more elaborate ones. A simple cone or cylinder mounted on a wooden rod can soon become a character. Add some accessories such as a hat or a few feathers and you can very easily create something which will give real pleasure.

We can follow this with a puppet made from different sized cones. It is important to begin with the design of the head which is the most important part of the puppet. Puppets made from cylinders are joined together by a narrow cylinder which passes from one part to the other. It can be decorated by cut out fluted paper round the neck. A wooden rod passing through will hold it all together.

Cone puppets are usually built up from the bottom, the pieces being stuck as the puppet is constructed. Once the structure has been completed the character of the puppet can be designed by sticking on accessories such as paper. For example a cat made out of cylinders and cones can be turned into a lion by sticking on pieces of curled paper.

To make puppets well it is important to be organised. You must have a good working space, and make sure your tools are readily to hand.

It is interesting to create the form of the puppets by cutting out a pattern. Draw a puppet on a piece of card, cut it out and then place it on another piece of card and draw round it. In the trunk of the body leave a slit about the thickness of the material used, halfway up the body. The two pieces can then be fitted together. This method gives an extra dimension to the head and the body. The puppet can then be painted. Other materials such as strips of paper, straw or cloth can then be added to increase the volume.

Here some simple fairies have been created from the cover of a cheese box and some paint. It is important that the children have a wide range of materials to choose from.

A cheese box for the head, a tube with two ends stuck on for the body. The other features are painted and glued on. Here we have a simple but effective lion.

Puppets can also be made from existing elements that already have their own volume. Packaging and boxes of all sorts and sizes can be used. It is important to find the shapes nearest to those you wish to represent. For example the top of a box of cheese can be the starting point for a puppet that needs to be round and fat. Square boxes are ideal for robots, while round boxes are nearer to humans and animals.

Knitted puppets have a dimension of a gentleness of form. Make a pattern taking into account the size of the puppet when it has been stuffed. You can use wool of different textures and colours. Sew it up and stuff them with small bits of material. Insert a piece of wire inside attached to a rod which will allow you to manipulate the puppets. Animal puppets should have two rods.

The use of existing elements prove a stimulation for the imagination. It is very simple to marry up the materials and the puppets created from them. Interesting materials are branches, corks, shells or metal and plastic bottle tops. In the case of branches, seeds and vegetables, it is the shape which will create the puppet. Polychrome will accentuate the original shape. Corks are a good material to use. They can be cut into any size, and filed down into any shape. You can stick them together with pins or pieces of wire.

It is the same with plastic bottles or bottle tops. To use this material it is important to have a good plastic glue. If it takes a while to dry, you can tie the pieces together with string or tape. This could even become a feature of the puppet!

The surface of plastic bottles can be changed by roughing them up with something like sandpaper. This can give it a very interesting appearance which can be coloured easily with paint or felt pen. For metal bottle tops you must have a metal glue.

Shells found on the beach can be used as a very attractive decoration. First it is important to have a good selection of shells, which will dictate the shape of the puppet. It is important that the puppets are small. In these puppets, as in the papier mâché puppets, the rod should be attached to the top of the puppet with modelling clay. The shells should be glued to modelling clay before it has dried.

Puppets larger than 15cm are made differently. They are made out of papier mâché and mounted on to a wooden rod. This is then covered with a layer of modelling clay to which the shells are stuck with glue. If there are any small gaps they can be filled with tiny shells, or painted. If you use either, use a colour which matches the shells, or a totally contrasting colour which will accentuate the unreal features of the shells.

Micky and Minnie Mouse have an important role in childhood fantasy. Here is a Micky Mouse made out of bottle tops.

Here you can see how easy it is to make a moving puppet out of cardboard, the limbs attached by paper clips. It is easier to design the whole body, and then cut it into pieces and attach the limbs separately.

Jumping jacks, flat moving puppets

The animation of puppets is a simulation of life. People have always been fascinated by the idea of bringing statues and robots to life. The jumping jack is a very important figure in the evolution of marionettes. A ridiculous figure made of cardboard or wood, whose limbs can be moved by using a pin. Its limbs move uncontrollably, hence the name Jumping Jack.

The jumping jack can be made facing front or in profile. Once the body has been designed the limbs and the head can be made. It is important to decide what sort of movement you want your puppet to have before you start to make it. If, for example, you wish to have a puppet with faster movements, you will need to make it out of thick cardboard or ply-wood cut out with a saw. Each moving portion

should be 3 or 4cm longer than normal. When all the pieces have been painted and cut out, you can carefully place them in position, and when satisfied, make a small hole and fix them together with a pin. Then you can fix a rod to the static part, and another to the moving limb. The idea is to move the main body of the puppet up and down, while perhaps the ears or the mouth can also be moved so that the puppet appears to listen to and speak to his audience. This is particularly effective in animal puppets. This effect is achieved by attaching a pin to each jaw. A piece of wire or elastic is attached between the two, thus making the jaw mobile. Once the movement stops, the jaw will then spring back into place.

Wire puppets. They must be simple and easy to handle. The quality of their style make for the simplicity of their movement.

Mr. Punch. A XIX century engraving. This famous character was the star of many plays in the puppet theatres at that time.

It is interesting to paint these puppets on both sides. The reverse side showing a different emotion. To make them easier to manipulate, these puppets have three rods, two of which are held in one hand.

The popularity of the Jumping Jack can be seen in many beautiful illustrations of the XIX century. Originating in Naples, Punch symbolises the mocking practical joker who triumphs not by force, but through laughter. Hunchbacked and wearing a brightly striped costume, with a ruff around the neck and a hat with two horns, he is familiar to all of us.

Several characters can be drawn together on the same piece of card. These can move together by simply using a strong piece of wire. Thus the arms of several characters can wave at the same time, or a troup of dancers can all lift their legs simultaneously.

An engraving of Pierrot dating from 1900. You can see how each wire is moved by a different finger.

Opposite, above
Sur le Pont d'Avignon. Characters cut out of cardboard and moved by a pulley. The shapes are stylized to emphasise the simplicity of the story.

Opposite, below
The Bellringer. The style is basic to emphasise the simplicity of the movement. The base is large in order that the scene can be seen in perspective.

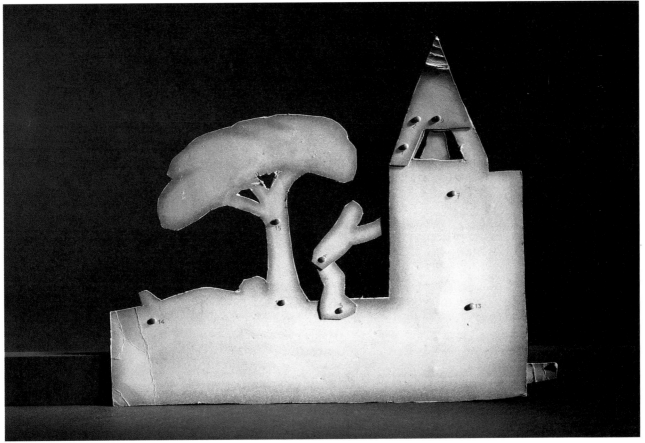

Rabbit and Bird.
Moving silhouettes.

Cardboard silhouettes,
moved by pulleys.
These are extremely
easy to manipulate.

Chinese shadow puppets

The many different methods of making characters by this technique are shown in this picture. The use of an oil lamp gives an added attraction to this game. Many kits such as this were sold, containing all the materials necessary to make one's own show.

A page explaining methods of making Chinese shadow puppets.

The child's design is the starting point for all work. It is important to retain the essence of the imaginative idea behind the design of the puppet.

Chinese shadow puppets were very fashionable in 1900. Here military figures are made out of cardboard, and mounted on rods.

This is an extremely old technique which originated in China, moved across Asia, Malaysia, Indonesia, and thence into Turkey and Greece. This type of show was extremely popular in Europe during the XVIII and XIX centuries. With the advent of the magic lanterns and later the cinema, its popularity waned. Lit from behind the shadows were projected onto a fine screen. They had the ability to move forward and backward, and to grow and become smaller. They were made out of a piece of cardboard attached to a baton by which they were moved. To make them look more realistic, holes were often cut in the eyes, the nostrils, the mouth, or in the accessories that they wore or carried. In this case, the puppets were made of a thinner card that could be pierced, and then reinforced with strips of cardboard or plywood. When it came to manipulation there were endless possibilities. A static face could suddenly open its mouth or eyes. The shape of the body could be changed, suddenly developing two heads or endless limbs. Crowds could gather and disperse. These were the very beginnings of cinema technique. To light indoors a simple light bulb was used, and if the show was to be outdoors at night they used a torch. It was easy to mount these shows. A large screen was all that was needed to allow several puppeteers to create many different characters.

61

AU BON MARCHÉ

L'OMBRE — LE PRÉDICATEUR

LITHOGRAPHIE ARTISTIQUE J MINOT & Cⁱᵉ EDITEURS, 5. RUE BÉRANGER   PARIS

The replacement of candles with oil lamps made the lighting more suitable for shadow
puppetry. This picture dating 1900 shows how children enjoyed exploring the possibilities
offered by shadow puppets.

The Great Fan. A luminous play for a Chinese shadow theatre.

A lid for a Chinese shadow theatre depicting the World Exhibition of 1900.

When making the puppet's head make sure that the clay is totally dry before you stick on the strips of paper.

When the heads are made out of modelling clay, exaggerate the features as the glued paper has a tendency to lessen the effect.

The head is stabilized by a cardboard cone large enough to insert a finger.

This cat is an excellent example of a puppet made from clay. It has well defined features which allow it to show its fraility, while at the same time dealing with any adversaries it should come across in the play.

Glove puppets

Puppet in painted wood. Sequins are often used to decorate the clothes, giving them a magical quality.

The different methods of making puppets dicate the different methods of manipulation. Glove puppets, which came originally from Italy, are very easy to animate. They are manipulated from below, the actor using his hand to enter the body of the puppet which is made of material. One finger moves the head, two more the hands, and the rest of the hand becomes the body of the puppet. Each puppeteer handles two puppets, taking care to change his voice and movements. The puppet heads for the professional theatre are mainly made of wood. This was particularly so in the past. A large piece of wood is trimmed on a lathe, then a cavity is cut out for the finger. It is then sculpted to acquire its features, which are then accentuated with paint. The puppeteer works with his arm in the air, and well hidden from his audience. He must always be careful to ensure that the base of the puppet is below the level of the bottom of the booth.

The heads of the puppets are made first, usually of wood, plaster, or papier mâché. We will start with a very simple method, and then progress to the more complex puppets. Make a cardboard cylinder just a little larger than a finger, or even simpler, take the centre from a roll of packaging or foil, and cut it to about 8 to 10cms. in length. Cover the top and place it inside a sock which has been stuffed. Pull it into shape and then tie it in position. Paint in the features, or they could be sewn on using buttons. Make a small sack to represent the body, cutting out two sleeves into which you can insert two painted cardboard hands.

1. The painted sock

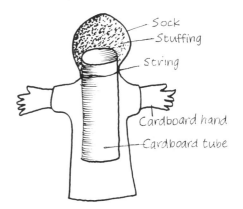

2. Papier Mâché.
Once the modelling clay is dry remove the stick and the stuffing.

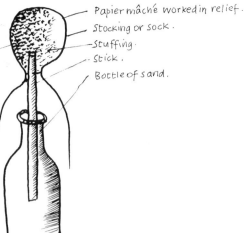

Papier mâché worked in relief.
Stocking or sock.
Stuffing.
Stick.
Bottle of sand.

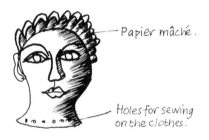

3. Papier mâché on modelling paste or clay. Three dimensional head covered with papier mâché.

Papier mâché.

Holes for sewing on the clothes.

Another slightly more elaborate method is to tie an old sock or stocking to a stick which has been filled with bits and pieces of material and pulled into the shape of a face. Fix the stick by tying it onto a chair leg or by putting it into a bottle filled with sand. This way you will have a steady base to work from. Prepare some pasted strips of paper and create the face in this way, allowing the eyes, the nose, the cheeks, the chin and the mouth to stand out. You could stick on some beads for the eyes, and some string or fur for the moustache and beard. Make sure that you use enough paper to give a strong consistency. When the head is dry you can untie the stick and remove the stuffing, leaving the head hollow.

The third method of making these puppets is to use modelling paste or clay, which gives you a better chance to accentuate the features. You then use the same papier mâché technique to make the head. When the head is dry you take out the clay from inside. Attach the clothes by sewing the material round the neck. These heads need to be painted all over with one colour and then dried before painting in the features. The clothes should be made of strong material and lots of bright colours should be used. The puppet can be brought to life by adding buttons, feathers, belts, ties and teeth, thereby making each one an individual.

Opposite, above
First cut out the shapes of animals on ordinary paper. Use this as a pattern to cut pieces of coloured materials matching up the seams. Felt, or pieces of furnishing fabric are particularly suited to this type of puppet.

Opposite, below
Mice, rabbits and ducks are part of the mythology of childhood. Children love familiar animals, and puppets give them the chance to have something to talk to, identify with, and invent stories together.

Rod and string puppets

pins

cardboard

Spring which
can be covered
with feathers,
paper, etc.

1. Manipulation. Two rods
which can both be held
in the same hand.

2. Manipulation
with two hands.

Movable joint
in the leg.

3. Extended character.

4. The enlarging and
moving of the arms.

5.
Moving
characters.

Movement allowed by pins.
Wire attached to three horses.

6. Scene moved
by rods.

Rod.

Rod puppets moved from below

The method for making the heads is the same as for glove puppets. For these puppets the size and movement of the hand does not have to be taken into consideration. The body can therefore be more well defined. The true shape and volume of the body can now be seen. The arms become thinner as they do not need to hold a finger. The arms must be attached loosely to the shoulders to allow for easy movement, made from cloth which is reinforced by a strong durable material, and stuffed with bits of cotton or chiffon. The rods must be as invisible as possible. They can be very fine in dimension and painted in a neutral colour.

Rod puppets moved from above

Rod puppets moved from above are one of the most ancient forms of puppetry. This method is animated by a main rod fixed to the centre of the head, another to the arm, while the other arm is attached to the main rod. These puppets were seen widely throughout Europe from the XVI to the XIX centuries. The rod is the centre of their being. They assume human form by having legs which appear to walk across the stage. These very human looking puppets were found as far apart as Sicily and South America where they were imported by the Spaniards. These ancient forms of puppetry told tales of chivalry and heroism. The puppeteer stood on a pedestal, or a bank if he was outdoors. The simple methods used to hide the puppeteer were a doorframe indoors or a piece of material draped between two trees for outdoor shows.

String puppets

The method of making these puppets is the same as other forms, but it is their manipulation which is infinitely more delicate. This is the supreme achievement in the art of puppetry. Here skill is vital. During the XVIII century the Italians were the main exponents of this art with their stories of Puncinella and the beginnings of the Commedia del Arte.

The feet, knees, arms and elbows are attached by string to a wooden cross which is held about 50 to 80cm above the puppet. The puppet then walks along the stage of the theatre. With this form we have reached a level of professionalism. However if you have a loggia or a raised platform, and the lighting, try making these puppets for yourself. When the play is finished, the simpler forms can assume the role of toys, while the works of art can be set up on a shelf as decoration. They allow the child by their very presence, to dream of the adventures in which he might take part.

6. Puppets for adults

Motivation and field of action

Many adults like puppets as an escape back into childhood. If for many years puppets have been exclusively the domain of children, this has not always been so. During the XVIII and the XIX centuries the Chinese shadow puppets were very much the prerogative of adults.

In 1887 the shadow puppet theatre of the Cabaret du Chat Noir was founded by Henri Rivier in Paris.

The famous designer, Caran d'Ache, designed the settings. It's success was enormous and later moved to the provinces. The writer, George Sand, created a puppet theatre at Nohan, which was much admired by Chopin and Delacroix. Many famous authors amused themselves at that time by writing and performing puppet plays, and it became extremely fashionable.

The Massacre Game. This game was played much like a puppet show, using the same techniques. The cast seem indifferent to each other

Characters from the Massacre Game. Wooden headed puppets representing a large number of craftsmen and legendary figures.

The approach is different, even opposite from that of children. The child takes an idea and a bundle of materials that he has gathered together, and spontaneously creates his story and characters. The adult is different. He has experience of life. He has lived through emotions and real life adventures. He knows the world, and he knows what he wants from life. The puppet for him is an evolving project. His puppet theatre is created for an audience. It is a means by which he can communicate with others, but using his puppets instead of having to stand and speak directly to the audience. Humour and farce are sometimes the only means open to him.

Puppets and their presentation are also a work of art. With patience and care it is possible to create, alone or with friends, a total spectacle. It is an ideal activity for those long winter evenings. The sense of achievement is tremendous. There is no need for a large working space, only the atmosphere of excitement when the play is finally performed. Most amateur puppeteers perform plays for their children or for their friends. The stories can be taken from the classical tales familiar to all, or new ones can be invented introducing characters familiar to the audience, such as neighbours, friends, or television characters.

Through this medium you have the world in your hand, you have at your disposal the means of releasing tension, and sharing an intimate secret with your audience. There are also the escapist stories of dream and poetry. The design and decor can play an important part in this sort of play. The puppets do not need to be elaborate. They can be made from serviettes, cardboard plates, or any other household bits and pieces, with features stuck on. If the story is interesting and amusing you will get your message across.

Some puppets are made by craftsmen such as silversmiths, cabinet makers or tailors in their spare time. These puppet shows can often be shown at special meetings or gatherings. The play is written in advance, and the parts distributed to be learned. There is often a prompter to make sure all goes well! These can take place anywhere from meeting halls, fairground booths, to gardens and fields.

Many children's books show illustration of Guignol. It is possible to buy texts for puppet plays, but children do enjoy improvisition.

It is important when children are working together that they have a central theme to work from. For example, familiar animals. This will ensure that as well as creating individually, the child is aware of the place of his puppet as part of a whole presentation.

Below
Chromolithography played an important part in making rod puppets and their decor. The era around 1900 relied particularly on this technique.

Left, below
Most mothers or grandmothers could knit a woollen puppet. They must be stuffed with light material so that the puppet can move easily.

Right, above
A knitted rod puppet. The more rods that are used the more complicated it becomes to manipulate them.

Right, below
A knitted owl. One could equally create this puppet out of an old sock or stocking, stuffed with straw, and then tied up and stuffed with material or straw, and painted.

Diversity of techniques

There are two different categories of puppet-maker among adults.
There are those who like the idea of puppets and enjoy manual
work, but who are not trained in any relevant skills. The other
category is those who have a certain expertise acquired from the
type of work they do. For instance a dentist or a plasterer who are
expert with plaster, or the skilled trades of locksmith, jeweller,
carpenter and tailor all have obvious advantages. Other pro-
fessions such as painting, acting and writing have their own
obvious skills to bring to the art of puppetry. The main principal
is not to copy the puppetry of children, but to do your own thing.
The basic technique however is not different. If you use water
based paints carefully you can make a spectacular effect, but oil
paints are particularly suitable for painting marionettes. If you go
to an art shop you can buy several tubes of basic colour which you
can then mix to make other colours, one or two strong brushes, a
fine brush for the features, and a little turpentine to thin down
the paint. If you have the remains of any household paint in the
cellar, do not throw it away. A couple of tubes of gold and silver
paint will give some added effect. When the paint is dry you can
varnish it with either oil paint varnish or wood varnish.

How to enjoy puppets

An interesting technique is to cut out and glue on the features from photographs. The simplest way of doing this is to paint the face entirely in basic colour. Then paint the cheeks pink, and the hair black or brown, before adding the features. Cut out the eyes, the nose, the mouth and the ears, and stick them into place. Following on from that, it is possible to cover the whole puppet with pieces cut out from photographs, giving it an element of realism.

You can of course use this method to add an element of surrealism to your puppet. A foot stuck on the face, an eye on the naval, and gloves instead of breasts. The caricature is emphasised by the colours of the photographs. You can play all sorts of games with these puppets, transforming politicians, famous film stars or even neighbours into any situation you desire.

Summing up the role of puppetry

All forms of entertainment have their part to play. Those involved have a need to fit characters into place, to create an atmosphere, and to direct the proceedings. The art of photography and cinema has made our society very aware of the visual and pictorial arts. In order to maintain their impact these techniques must be constantly improved.

Where illustrations and pictures gave puppets their original inspiration, the puppet gave inspiration to those who developed the cinema. The puppet therefore takes its place between the moving illustration and the cinema. Clubs for film and photography often liase with members of puppet making clubs and work together.

In the theatre we find the actors become like fully grown puppets, and puppets are often used alongside actors, each playing their part in enhancing the whole performance.

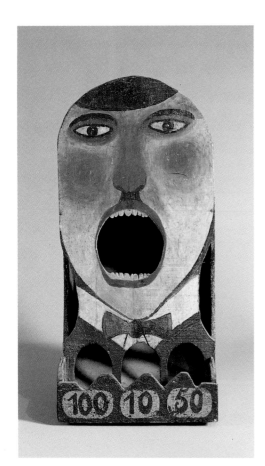

Processions, masked balls, and carnival floats, often carry a giant puppet. Some can be operated by one person, while others need several people to animate them. They are sometimes animated mechanically, the movement being controlled manually, or using a concealed motor.

The papier mâché technique used is the same as for smaller puppets however the frame for these larger puppets is different. Instead of using clay or modelling paste, a large frame is made of slats of wood or fashioned out of thin wire such as chicken wire. It is then covered with strips of paper glued on until it reaches the required thickness. When it is dry, it can be painted and decorated.

At carnivals the floats can be seen representing many different ideas and styles. They are often beautifully decorated with cut flowers and painted accessories. There are different puppets manifested at these carnivals, some traditional such as Punch or Guignol, others created specially for the theme of the carnival, and others created to caricature the figures familiar in our every-day life.

The puppet creates a life that we can recognise, and becomes more important in our life as the techniques become more diverse. For example, the television programme 'Spitting Image' allows us to comment on, and laugh at those who are responsible for shaping our lives. Long life, and quality of life to puppets, and as Guignol concludes 'I am as good as anybody'!

Left, above
The puppet theatres and the mobile games played extensively in the late XIX century, were very similar in the way they were made, and in the characters used.

Left, below
Another example of a game called 'Pass the Ball'. The character was made from papier mâché and varnished paint, just the same as puppets.

Opposite
A clown wearing a moon and riding an ass. (Scene from a puppet play).

Below
Carnivals gave birth to the giant papier mâché puppet. Framed in wood or fine wire, they are painted and dressed in the usual manner.